Copyright Law

A Beginner's Guide To Copyright Law And Protection

By
Jasmine Baker

Copyrights Notice

No part of this book can be transmitted or reproduced in any form including print, electronic, photocopying, scanning, mechanical, or recording without prior written permission from the author.

All information, ideas, and guidelines presented here are for educational purposes only. This book cannot be used to replace information provided with the device. All readers are encouraged to seek professional advice when needed.

While the author has taken utmost efforts to ensure the accuracy of the written content, all readers are advised to follow the information mentioned herein at their own risk. The author cannot be held responsible for any personal or commercial damage caused by misinterpretation of information or improper use of the information.

Legal Notice

The Publisher has strived to be as accurate and complete as possible in the creation of this report, notwithstanding the fact that he does not warrant or represent at any time that the contents within are accurate due to the rapidly changing nature of the Internet.

The Publisher will not be responsible for any losses or damages of any kind incurred by the reader whether directly or indirectly arising from the use of the information found in this report.

This report is not intended for use as a source of legal, business, accounting or financial advice. All readers are advised to seek services of competent professionals in legal, business, accounting, and finance field.

No guarantees of success and/or income are made. Reader assumes responsibility for use of information contained herein. The author reserves the right to make changes without notice. The Publisher assumes no responsibility or liability whatsoever on the behalf of the reader of this report.

Table of Contents

Introduction 1

Chapter One: Understanding Copyright? 3
Copyright Explained? 5
Resources 14

Chapter Two: 7 Myths about Online Copyright 15
What can and can't be copyrighted? 18
Resources 24

Chapter Three: Plagiarism, Copyright, and Fair Use 25
Copyright Infringement in the Digital World 29
Resources 31

Chapter Four: How to Deal with Copyright Issues 32
What Are the Most Common Forms of Intellectual Property? 34
Resources 38

Chapter Five: In Copyright Infringement Cases, How Do You Respond To Settlement Letters? 39
Copyright Registration's Benefits 40
Resources 44

Chapter Six: Top 10 Reasons to Register Your Copyright . 45
How to Avoid Copyright Violations 48
Resources 51

Chapter Seven: Protect Your Work With Copyrights 52
Ensuring That You Own Your Content's Copyright 54
Resources 58

Chapter Eight: How to Acquire Copyright for a Book 60

How to Copyright a Book - 4 Tips to Protect Your Novel 62

Resources 65

Chapter Nine: Tips to Choose The Best Copyright Lawyer 66

5 Ways To Stay Away From Copyright Infringement On Social Media 68

Resources 70

Chapter Ten: How To Obtain Copyright Permission? 71

Resources 76

Conclusion 77

Introduction

Copyright is a legal right that is automatically granted to the creator of any creative work. This could be a single individual, a group of people, or a corporation. The owner of copyright has complete control over how their work is used.

The sole right to copy, distribute, perform, broadcast, or modify a work belongs to the copyright owner.

Anyone wishing to duplicate a copyrighted work must first obtain permission from the owner of the copyright, or check to see if the owner has granted permission through a license.

There are various exceptions that allow copyrighted content to be used without the owner's permission. These are only applicable in very narrow situations. Some of these exceptions apply to educational purposes, but you must still adhere to specific guidelines.

Copyright is granted for a specific amount of time. This can last anything from a few decades to several centuries. When works are no longer protected by copyright, they become freely available in the public domain. However, there may be some restrictions on reuse.

The legal right of the owner of intellectual property is known as copyright. Simply put, copyright refers to the ability to duplicate. This means that only the original producers of items, as well as anybody they provide permission to, have the sole right to replicate the work.

For a set period of time, copyright law grants authors of creative work the exclusive right to use and duplicate that material, after which the copyrighted item becomes public domain.

This book gives you a step-by-step guide to copyright knowledge, as well as resources.

Chapter One: Understanding Copyright?

A copyright is a set of rights that are automatically granted to someone who creates an original work of authorship, such as a book, music, film, or piece of software. These rights include the ability to duplicate the work, create derivative works, distribute copies, and publicly perform and show it.

To visualize how these rights can be used or leased, consider them as a bundle of sticks, with each stick representing one of these rights. Each "stick" has the right to be kept by the copyright owner, to be transferred individually to one or more individuals, or to be transferred collectively to one or more people. In a nutshell, copyright gives the owner control over how his or her copyrighted works are distributed to the public.

The basis for copyright protection is found in the United States Constitution. The Framers considered that granting authors limited exclusive rights to their publications would "advance the progress of science and useful arts."

The basic goal of copyright is to encourage and compensate authors to create new works by providing property rights and making those works available for public enjoyment. According to the argument, by allowing creators certain exclusive rights that allow them to safeguard their creative works from theft, they benefit economically while the public benefits from creative works that would not otherwise be developed or distributed.

While copyright legislation is meant to benefit the general public by providing access to creative works, it's crucial to remember that creators are under no duty to make their copyrighted works available.

The rights granted to copyright owners are, of course, subject to various limits. Under certain circumstances, anyone can use a work without first obtaining permission from the copyright owner or paying the copyright owner.

A work must meet three essential characteristics in order to be protected by copyright. The task must be completed as follows:

To be original, a work must simply be made independently. To put it another way, it can't be replicated. There is no requirement that the work be fresh, unique, innovative, or ingenious (as under patent law). To achieve the originality criteria, a work just needs to show a minimal level of ingenuity. Only a few projects fall short of the required level of inventiveness.

A Work of Authorship: A work must be a product of creative expression that falls within a category of copyrightable subject matter to qualify as a work of authorship for the purposes of copyright protection. Literary works, musical works, motion films and other audiovisual works, derivative works, compilations, and other works are all examples of copyrightable subject matter.

A work must be fixed in a physical medium of expression to meet the fixation requirement. Protection is immediately applied to qualified work after it is completed. A work is deemed fixed if it is sufficiently persistent or stable to allow it to be observed, reproduced, or otherwise communicated for more than a brief period of time.

These three standards are not difficult to meet in terms of copyright protection. In fact, unlike the standards for patent or trademark protection, relatively few works that falls under the purview of copyright fail to meet all three of these criteria. To get copyright protection, a copyright owner does not need to register his or her work with the United States Copyright Office or place a copyright notice on the work.

A copyrighted work is generally protected for the author's lifetime plus another seventy years. Copyright protection is awarded for collaborative works for the life of the last living joint creator plus an additional 70 years. Works created for hire, as well as anonymous and pseudonymous works, are protected for 95 years from the date of first publication or 120 years from the date of creation, whichever comes first. When a copyrighted work's term of protection expires, the work becomes public domain.

Copyright Explained?

Artists, writers, innovators, and entrepreneurs...in fact, creative and business people from all backgrounds have found they've had misconceptions about what copyright is, how it works, for what types of creative work, and what it can accomplish for them at some point or another.

So, let's get started, starting with the most basic issues about copyright: what is it and why does it exist in the first place?

Let's begin with the second question.

What is the purpose of copyright?

Consider the following scenario: you decide to build a cottage of your own design. It's a lovely Tudor-style house with a thatched roof, a modest, well-kept garden, and a stunning view of rolling, luscious green hills with breathtaking sunsets in the evening. Imagine someone learning about your one-of-a-kind, very appealing cottage one day and moving in while you're away. You return home to find you can't get back in, and the squatter inside claims ownership of your property, even claiming to have constructed it, and worse, they've started renting out the rear bedroom for a good price. To top it off, they're now building identical cottages to your design down the road in order to sell and profit even more. Imagine there was no law in place to allow you to reclaim possession of your property, and you had no way of stopping the usurper or obtaining reparation from them.

Apply this clumsy example to creativity, and you'll see why copyright exists.

I appreciate how the Irish Patents Office describes the nature of copyright on their website:

"First, individuals who develop intellectual works or invest in their creation and distribution have a human right to receive a fair return on their ingenuity and effort.

Second, unless artists' and investors' rights to a fair return are protected, the community as a whole would suffer as a result of the fact that many of these works will not be created or developed."

Creativity and innovation are the engines that propel our civilization forward. Creators, on the other hand, need to eat, live, earn money, be recognized for their work, and have the motivation to keep going when things become bad. As a result, **Copyright** exists to make this possible and to assist innovators in monetizing their ideas. Copyright exists to stimulate creativity and assist creative people in making a living from it. Copyright exists because it is both creative and commercially beneficial.

If a writer gets money from their work, they will be able to continue to write. If an artist receives money through the licensing and manufacture of images of artwork, they will have enough money to invest in more initiatives. Copyright also exists to promote creativity and prosperity, both for society as a whole and for the individual who is creating.

If you start with text, you basically bind the hands of the creative behind their backs. Imagine a world that is culturally, creatively, industrially, and economically starved as a result of innovators not being rewarded for their efforts and not having the power to safeguard their usage.

Let's put my cottage analogy into context now, shall we? You're a creative person, aren't you? Imagine that every time you developed something, someone could come along and replicate it, claim it as their own, and most likely profit from it, with no fear of repercussions because their activities were not criminal by law. Wouldn't you soon abandon your creative endeavors? What's the use of all that effort if someone else gets the credit and the reward?

Fortunately for us, this is not the case in reality. Let us read what the Irish Patents Office says again: "...it is a human right to receive a fair return for their ingenuity and investment." I'll say it again: well said.

As a result, copyright exists.

But what is copyright, exactly?

Copyright is defined as...

If you think about it, my crude cottage analogy essentially shows what copyright is: a property right. But a property right that applies to products of the human mind... of our intelligence, rather than land, buildings, or automobiles. Literary, theatrical, musical, artistic, or filmic works are examples of creative products.

And what can this "intellectual property" be used for, right?

Copyright, on the other hand, has some similar but also distinct rights from other types of property rights, allowing the copyright owner (or owners) to:

Copy, lend and distribute their work

Allow others to utilize the copyright owner's work by granting formal authorization.

Adapt their work or give others permission to do so (e.g. adapt a book into a movie).

They can sell their original work - their intellectual property - to others, and, more significantly, they can...

Have the authority to prevent unjust violation of those rights by third parties, such as the unauthorized copying and exploitation of the copyright owner's work, as well as...

Where income loss has been discovered, obtain reimbursement in the form of compensation or damages for infringement.

This is true whether a copyright owner's work has been published, displayed, or otherwise made available to the public for consumption.

But it doesn't stop there...

Copyright's Moral Rights

A copyrighted work's creator and commissioner are also entitled to other rights related to their work under copyright. These are referred to as "Moral Rights":

The right to be identified as the author (or artist, or photographer, or musician, or director, or anything) and to have their work erroneously attributed to them.

The right to have their work not be subjected to disparaging treatment (alteration, re-arrangement, or deletion) by others; "derogatory treatment" is defined as when the resulting work is mutilated, distorted, or can harm the creator/reputation.

When it comes to some photographs and films, you have the right to privacy (e.g. a commissioner of private photos has the right not to have them published or exhibited to the public where the photos become copyright works)

Here are some examples of the three points mentioned above:

I've established my moral right to be named as the article's author, as well as my legal right to do so (3). If this were a fictional book that was converted into a film, I would have the right to be recognized in the film as the author of the source novel unless you waived that right. In contrast, Alan Moore's now-legendary dissatisfaction with the portrayal of his graphic novels in film adaptations, and how he believes they have reflected poorly on his original work, has driven him to demand that his name be removed from the credits of films like Watchmen.

If someone else knowingly and deliberately credited J K Rowling's Harry Potter series of novels as my work rather than hers, both she and I could stop it due to false attribution.

If I believed a third party (an editor, a publisher, or a printer) had done a hatchet job on all my hard work throughout the editing of this book, I would have the right to not only express my displeasure with the treatment, but also to halt it.

Finally, the professional portraits of my significant other and me that we paid for hang on the walls of our home... and nowhere else without our permission.

Do you know how Moral Rights work?

On the other hand, moral rights cannot be asserted when copyrighted works are computer programs or computer-generated material (produced without human interaction), or when a typeface design is involved. The Moral Right hasn't been infringed if the creator/author hasn't asserted their right to be identified as the creator/author if that right applies. Furthermore, you will not have this right if the creator/author works for an employer who owns or will own the copyright to the work you generate (more on this "Work Made For Hire" later).

Who owns the copyright?

Now that we've established the "what" and "why" of copyright, let's investigate the "who": who is this "copyright owner" I've mentioned:

The individual or persons who developed the copyrighted work are known as the copyright owner.

You've probably figured it out by now.

As explained above, under copyright law, creative are usually the first people to be granted ownership of copyright over the work they've made.

(7) As a result, if you've created a copyrighted work, you're the exclusive proprietor of that copyrighted work.

Let's be clear: no one else has these rights except you, the creator of the copyrighted work; not your mother, partner, or sweet Mrs Miggins down the street. (Not even her, for that matter.) They're all yours, and they're all yours alone (unless the created work has been a collaborative effort).

Those rights will not belong to anybody else unless and until you, as the rights owner (also known as "rights holder"), grant permission to use, license, or give away/sell, or transfer those rights.

Doesn't it sound appealing? It seems to work for me.

However, having stated that

Then there's ownership, and then there's ownership, and then there's ownership, and then there's ownership, and

People often get the wrong end of the stick when it comes to copyright ownership, so now that I've defined what it is, I thought it'd be useful to define what it isn't.

DVDs, books, and CDs are all over the place where you live now, and you own them, right? You did pay a lot of money for them, right? Yes, you did. So you're the one who owns them.

But does this imply that you own the copyright to those products?

You don't, of course.

The copyright is retained by the author and/or the publisher/distributor. There's a distinction to be made between having a copy of a copyrightable work and owning the copyright to that work. When you buy a CD, for example, you're purchasing ownership of that CD copy of that recording artist's album, not ownership of the master recordings or the right to make copies of the CD you bought.

If the work was created by more than one author or creator, then joint copyright ownership applies. Songwriting partnerships are a classic example, whereby they each become joint copyright owners by virtue of co-writing a song.

Then there's the matter of being hired to do some work.

Have you been hired? Make a copyright check.

We've all worked as employees, and many of us have also been employed as independent contractors. And I guarantee you that during that time, we put something together, wrote something, or drew something for our employer. Is this to say that copyright became ours as a result of what I've stated above?

Certainly not.

Because, if we prepared this work as part of our job duties, or if it was commissioned from us, or if we're part of a project team, or if we're developing something under a "work created for hire" agreement, the copyright will almost certainly belong to our employers, not to us.

So, are you working right now and creating things that you thought you had the rights to? Then go over the employment contract you signed with your boss. There are undoubtedly provisions in there that address the issue of ownership. Are you commissioning work from others, or are you commissioning work from others? Then take a look at the purchase orders or agreements you've signed. Are there any stipulations in the terms and conditions that address intellectual property rights for people you hire, ensuring that you own those rights once you pay?

So, that's what copyright is, what it's for, and who gets to use it.

Resources

The U.S. Copyright Office

Copyright FAQ from the Copyright Office

The Law from the Copyright Office

Patent, Trademarks and Copyright from the National Paralegal College

Copyright Information for Educators and Librarians

Chapter Two: 7 Myths about Online Copyright

Copyright is one of the most misunderstood topics on the internet. Copyright difficulties arise in both e-mail and Web site content. For some reason, like with so many things online, there is an erroneous belief that everything goes or that the entire internet is "public domain." Many people are learning the hard way that copyright is the law when it comes to protecting intellectual content. Copyright laws can be enforced online, and they are.

No, I am not a lawyer. I don't even pretend to be one on TV. But, based on my experience guiding customers for over a decade about the risks associated with using other people's work, I can assist you avoid such pitfalls. Hopefully, our effort will save you the trouble of discovering the hard way that copyright exists online.

"I can right-click, save, and use anything I see online." This is a great example of "just because you can," not "just because you should!" Someone somewhere developed those graphics or files. When that file was created, they legally acquired the copyright. You have no right to download that material or graphic and use it as you want without the express consent of the creators. This rule does not have any exceptions. Before stealing content from another site to use on your own, always ask the owner first.

"I can use their stuff on my site as long as I note the author's name." You still need to acquire the author's permission to post their work on your site, even if you're being courteous and providing credit where credit is due. The author may not want their information to be placed elsewhere other than their own site, or they may not approve of your site as a forum for their information; it is their decision, not yours. You do not have permission just because you desire to provide credit. Before putting content on your site, always ask the site owner if you can use it.

"I can link to visuals on other websites and have them appear on my own." Okay, so you didn't really download the graphic and upload it to your website, but the bottom line remains the same if you're exhibiting someone else's work on your site without their permission. Furthermore, you are displaying their files on your site utilizing their server's resources.

"I can use frames on my site to display pages from other websites." Many website owners do not allow their pages to be framed within another site because it creates the idea that the information was developed by the other site. Many people do this unintentionally so they don't have to drive visitors away from their site to get the information they seek. Others do so to give the idea that the content was created by them. A better approach is to build a new window to open when you link to the content you want, ensuring that your site remains accessible to your visitors.

"I don't need their permission if I merely quote a fraction of their work and link to them." It would behoove you, once again, to have permission to do so. Using only bits of the author's content can create the false idea of the author's entire content, which is at best inaccurate. If you want to quote any written work in its entirety or in part, you must first obtain permission.

"I hold the copyright on the visuals that I hire someone to design for my Web site." Certainly not. Unless your contract with the graphic artist expressly indicates that upon payment, all of their rights are transferred to you in their entirety, you most likely only have an exclusive license to use those images. Furthermore, full copyright would set you back considerably more than mere exclusivity! The fact is that the author owns the copyright as soon as something is made, whether it is written or drawn. That is the law. Only a formal legally binding agreement signed by the work's creator stating that they are transferring their rights to you can transfer copyright. It's not enough to say you own something because you paid for it.

"Once an email is sent, it is not copyright protected." E-mail is a literary work that is protected by the author's copyright once it is created. This means that an e-mail addressed to you privately cannot be made public. Private e-mails cannot be posted on your site, message boards, or blog without the author's express permission. Just because you received an e-mail as a private communication does not mean you now own it and can do whatever you want with it. Furthermore, e-mail sent to a group of individuals, such as on a mailing list or Newsgroup, is not available for reposting, copying, or any other use without the author's express and written permission.

What's the bottom line when it comes to copyright on the internet?

Don't assume that just because you can, you can use, repost, or take something you find online. Always inquire first!

What can and can't be copyrighted?

Copyright refers to the legal right to control copies and distribute one's work. The owner of the copyright can temporarily prohibit others from copying, modifying, or distributing their work. Its goal is to encourage creators to keep creating so that the general public can profit from their efforts. Knowing those two things makes it easier to understand the laws about what can and can't be copyrighted.

Only three things are required to copyright something: **(1) fixation, (2) originality, and (3) expression.**

(1) Fixation: A creative idea must be kept for an indefinite period of time. A song, for example, must be notated on paper or transcribed into tape or CD to be protected. That song's live performance will not be protected.

(2) Expression: The necessity for expression goes hand in hand with the requirement for fixation. Although ideas cannot be copyrighted, the "expression" of an idea can. The notion of making a film about a sophisticated, British superspy who employs quirky technology, for example, cannot be copyrighted, but the James Bond films, which are the manifestation of that idea, may.

(3) Originality: To be deemed an author's product, creative work must achieve a fundamental level of originality. Facts, short phrases, titles, and other items that are not direct reproductions of someone else's work are not copyrighted. The names and addresses in a phonebook, for example, cannot be copyrighted, but the photo on the front cover can.

To completely comprehend these three prerequisites, you'll need to dig a little deeper.

(1) Fixation

You must fix your work "in a physical medium" to acquire copyright protection. That is to say, in order to copyright your music, you must first record it and write down the lyrics. Your story must be written on paper or saved in a word processor to be copyrighted.

Your music is not protected by copyright if you play it live for a friend without recording it, notating it, or writing down the words. You won't get copyright protection for your song until it's in a state where it may be replicated, regardless of its quality.

Work that is "sufficiently persistent or stable to permit it to be perceived, reproduced, or otherwise communicated for a time of more than transitory length" is referred to as "fixed." A sandcastle or ice sculpture that you work on all day, for example, is unlikely to be considered fixed, and hence is not copyrightable. However, if you photograph your sandcastle or ice sculpture, the picture and design of the sandcastle can be legally protected because it is fixed in a reproducible medium other than your own memory.

(2) Expression

Consider requesting a movie recommendation from a buddy. You tell a friend that you want to attend a film about a slick federal spy who uses gadgets and attracts women. That synopsis is merely a suggestion.

That person's manifestation of that thought would be if they handed you a James Bond DVD. That person may also give you a DVD of xXx, its sequel, xXx: State of the Union, or any of the Austin Powers films. Those, too, would be representations of the same concept.

Expressions are protected under the Copyright Act. It doesn't cover "ideas," "procedures," "processes," "systems," "methods of operation," "concepts," "principles," or "discoveries."

When you consider that copyright laws exist only for the benefit of the public, the purpose of the Act's delineation becomes logical. The law requires anyone interested in writing about government spies to actually write about spies. Someone who is just thinking about writing a novel does not benefit the public. As a result, if someone does not express their thoughts, the public does not benefit. Therefore, the idea cannot be protected as a copyrighted notion.

If ideas were protected, anyone who came up with an interesting, memorable character for a film or book would be barred from creating a character that was similar. The same may be true of well-known stories and settings. Everything in the human experience would be copyrighted fast if these could be protected. After all, some say that there are only 36 potential story plots that can be told, and that each story is only a variant of one of those 36 storylines.

When you contemplate the concept of parallel independent invention, it becomes clearer: copyright rules protect your specific expression of an idea, but they don't stop someone else from independently inventing that same expression.

Assume you're a poet in Brooklyn, New York, and you've just written a 10-line masterpiece that you've been working on at the coffee shop every day for the past year. Meanwhile, while waiting for his drink in a pub 3,000 miles away in California, Average Joe writes the same poetry on the back of a napkin, word for word. Both of you would have full copyright protection on your poetry because you both independently thought of it and created the expression without being affected by the other's work. It makes no difference who wrote it first.

(3) Originality

"Everything has been done before," as the cliché goes. As I previously stated, some wise people believe that there are only 36 stories that can be recounted. Everything we've ever seen or read is a retelling of one of these tales.

The law on copyright takes this into account by requiring a low level of originality. Though no one can say for sure what is and isn't original, examples from previous cases can provide useful insight.

A photograph on a phonebook's front cover is definitely an original work. However, as the Supreme Court concluded in Feist Publications, Inc. v. Rural Telephone Service Co., a list of names and addresses listed alphabetically in a phonebook is not original. The line between protected originality and non-protected unoriginality is somewhere between the two cases.

The law also recognizes that some creative works, particularly those in genres like science fiction and westerns, include a lot of common features that aren't always copyrightable. Westerns are full of horses, saloons, and quick-shooting cowboys, while science fiction stories are full of spacecraft, aliens, or nasty space soldiers. Some aspects of these types of stories are so formulaic that they aren't covered by copyright. These non-copyrightable portions of works are referred to as scenes-a-faire under the law.

Finally, it's worth emphasizing that when it comes to originality, the law isn't concerned with the quality of the work. A child's crayon drawing is just as copy able as a professional painter's masterpiece. Low-budget pornography is equally as innovative as art films or big-budget summer blockbusters, and therefore deserves copyright protection.

To summarize, if something satisfies the common sense definition of creative labor, it is more than likely to satisfy the originality requirement.

Putting everything together

Titles, short phrases, facts, and utilitarian language, in general, are not protected by copyright. This makes sense because they are either too similar to ideas or not unique enough to meet the standards of copyright law. This means that even if someone spends a significant amount of time and mental energy creating a title, I am free to reproduce it and use it in my own work in whatever way I see fit.

Facts

The law of copyright protects a person's expression but not their facts. Under copyright law, a person who discovers a fact about the world (such as a biologist discovering a truth about human cellular structures, a historian discovering a fact about Napoleon's life, or a journalist discovering hidden information about a news event) is not the author of that fact. Rural Telecommunications Service. [499 U.S. 340, 347 (1991).] That person hasn't spoken anything to cause the fact, and a fact of the world doesn't require any creative creativity.

To put it another way, facts can be uncovered, but this is not the same as authorship.

Consider this scenario: You're a historian who has spent your life attempting to prove through the archeological record that Genghis Khan was a peace-loving Mongolian philosopher rather than an aggressive Mongolian warlord. After a decade of combing the Mongolian Steppes for archeological evidence, you finally find proof that your hypothesis is correct. All of this is published in a thorough biography of Genghis Khan's life that makes history.

Because you merely learned a non-protectable historical truth, a movie producer would not have to pay you a dollar if he wanted to film a movie about Genghis Khan being an ancient peace-loving beatnik, utilizing all of the information you provide in your book.

However, if a movie producer wanted to make a film based on your biography (using lines from your book or the structure of your book), he'd need your consent because he'd be using the rights to your "expression" of the historical facts you learnt.

Even if you independently created the fact or are the only person who knows about it, it cannot be protected.

Titles

Individual work titles are not protected by copyright or trademark law. Unfair competition rules are the only way for titles to be protected.

Phrases are not protected by copyright legislation.

Short sentences, on the other hand, may be protected.

Resources

[The Digital Millennium Copyright Act from the Copyright Office (pdf file)](#)

[Copyright Term Extension Act from the Copyright Office (pdf file)](#)

[Know your copyrights](#)

[Copyright Renewal Database a Google project](#)

[How to Investigate the Copyright Status of a Work from the Copyright Office](#)

Chapter Three: Plagiarism, Copyright, and Fair Use

You've fallen in love with a poem you saw on the internet and want to include it in your book. Is that, however, plagiarism? You'd want to paraphrase a paragraph from a book, but you're not sure if you need permission. When do you need permission to utilize a copyrighted work and what constitutes fair usage?

I constantly see people on the Internet stealing from others by reposting their articles, tales, or images. You must obtain permission before posting someone else's information on your website or using it in your book. There are exceptions, such as public domain and fair use, but it's always better to be safe. Before you decide to utilize someone else's property and risk enraging that individual and potentially face a lawsuit, consider the following:

1. 1. Do I really need this fact, poem, comic, or whatever it is? Will my book or website still work if I don't have it?
2. 2. Is this a public domain item?
3. 3. Can I use a portion of it under fair use regulations if it isn't in the public domain?
4. 4. Is it possible to alter or rework the work before republishing it?
5. 5. Is giving credit sufficient?

Let's take a closer look at each of these concerns.

Is this information really necessary? Will my book or website still work if I don't have it?

I practically promise that you can do without the knowledge, documents, poetry, cartoons, or whatever it is in any scenario. Why would you want to utilize someone else's property to demonstrate your own? You can either hire your own cartoonist or artist, or you can create your own poetry. If you're unable to do so, search the public domain for one. If you absolutely must incorporate something that is copyrighted, you must be willing to pay for it. You'll need to ask the owner or his or her heir for permission, and you'll almost certainly have to sign a document committing to exclusively use it for the purposes for which you've been given permission. You'll almost always have to pay to use it, especially if you're using it for commercial purposes, such as in a book you want to sell, and you'll almost certainly have to spend a lot of money for it—hundreds of dollars or more is not uncommon. Is it really necessary to offer it in your book or on your website at that price?

Is this a public domain item?

What exactly is the public domain? It varies depending on the country and the type of work. In the United States now, copyright is for life plus 70 years, so if I died tomorrow, in the year 2012, whatever I wrote would be copyrighted until 2082. However, because copyright regulations were less stringent in the past, certain works may have expired copyrights. You're usually safe if an author or artist has been dead since 1941 or before, but it never hurts to double-check. Furthermore, just because an old work, such as "Don Quixote," is in the public domain does not imply that a modern translation of it is.

What is "fair use"?

Even if a work isn't in the public domain, you can normally use a little portion of it if it's suitable, such as a quote or section that doesn't exceed a page. However, despite its short length, a short work like a poem cannot be utilized in its whole because you will be using the entire work, but you may be allowed to quote a verse or stanza from it. Even so, it's preferable to be safe and get permission to quote from the work in your book or on your website in such circumstances. The purpose of its use, whether commercial or charitable, whether the quote is used to promote the work, such as in a book review, or whether your use of it will harm sales of someone else's book because you provide too much information from it, are all factors that go into determining what constitutes fair use.

To go straight to the source, here are some instances of fair use from the 1961 Report of the Register of Copyrights on the General Revision of the United States Copyright Law:

"quotation of short passages in a scholarly or technical work for illustration or clarification of the author's observations; quotation of excerpts in a review or criticism for purposes of illustration or comment; quotation of short passages in a review or criticism for purposes of illustration or comment; use of some of the parodied work's content in a parody; a brief synopsis of a speech or article in a news report; A library's reproduction of a portion of a work to replace a damaged copy; A teacher's or student's reproduction of a small part of a work to illustrate a lesson; Incidental and fortuitous reproduction of a work located at the scene of an event being reported in a newsreel or broadcast;

reproduction of a work in legislative or judicial proceedings or reports. " http://www.copyright.gov/fls/fl102.html

When borrowing someone else's work, there are always fine lines to be navigated. Even if you're confident it qualifies under fair use regulations, if the work isn't in the public domain, it's advisable to ask for permission to use it, and if that seems impractical, consult an attorney.

Is it possible to alter or reword the work before republishing it?

You may summarize a work and provide acknowledgment to the source, but you may never rewrite someone else's work and pass it off as your own, or even as theirs when it is rewritten. Even if you paraphrase an idea, it is still the intellectual property of someone else, thus credit must be given where credit is due.

Is it enough to give credit?

No, giving credit isn't enough. You'll also need permission to reprint unless it's in the public domain, as mentioned above. Whether it's an author, publication, artist, or another website, you must always provide credit to the owner. It's typically enough to say who the work's original creator or copyright holder is. Give the title and name of the poet if it's a poem. You can say, "George Smith states in his book 'My Brilliant Ideas,' that:" Depending on your book or website, you might want to consult a style handbook for the proper way to reference a source. The "Chicago Manual of Style" is the standard style manual for most publications; others, such as the "Publication Manual of the American Psychological Association" (APA style) or the "Christian Writers Manual of Style," exists based on the type of book you're writing. If you do get permission to republish copyrighted material, make sure you ask the owner how you're supposed to cite that permission.

Always check to see if a work is copy-lifted and provide credit where credit is due. Then you won't have to worry about issues like fair use violations, copyright infringements, or plagiarism later on.

Copyright Infringement in the Digital World

It is not illegal to download files from the internet, but it is illegal to download files for free that you would normally have to pay for. The issue of piracy arises when copyright owners do not receive the compensation they are owed.

Piracy is defined as the illegal copying and sale of copyrighted materials, although many individuals believe it is unimportant because no one is harmed. In truth, the global economy has been impacted by the evolution of piracy from burning CDs and DVDs to digital copying. Piracy of a physical copy or unauthorized streaming has a negative impact on artists' livelihoods.

The quality of pirated copies isn't always good.

The majority of the time, illicit copies do not match the quality of the original. The quality of a pirated movie may be poor because it was recorded with a camcorder in the back of a cinema. At times, the content may be grainy or black and white. On the other hand, copies acquired via the internet may abruptly stop at some points, and the sound quality may be quite faint and muffled.

Easy digital access

Because of the convenience, downloading directly from a computer has become popular among internet users. Even with the growing number of sites that provide legal downloads, file-sharing networks continue to provide free access to copyrighted files. And it's unfortunate that so many people are involved in some type of piracy, whether it's through streaming, downloading, or buying counterfeit DVDs the old-fashioned way.

Piracy, in any scenario, costs the entertainment business money. It is a form of theft from the art world's enterprises. People must realize that there is no such thing as a free lunch. When a user streams unauthorized content, pirate sites make money through subscription fees or advertising. The owners of these websites profit from the distribution of copyrighted materials that they do not own and are not authorized to disseminate.

How can the problem be minimized?

It has always been difficult to persuade internet service providers to assist in the fight against piracy and the detection of copyright infringements. It would necessitate content owners educating individuals and private entities about the value of copyright and encouraging them to support legal ways to consume content, such as going to the movies or subscribing to Netflix and other video-on-demand services.

Piracy is difficult to eradicate, although it can be decreased. Besides, with all of the new technology being released, all we have to do is keep up. There are also organizations that utilize software to detect copyright infringements to aid in the fight against piracy.

Resources

Registering Your Work

Forms from the Copyright Office

Obtaining Permissions

The Copyright Clearance Center

The Digital Object Identifier System a plan to identify works on the net and link users with copyright holders

The American Society of Composers Authors and Publishers

Broadcast Music, Inc. (BMI)

Chapter Four: How to Deal with Copyright Issues

More ideas and products are being conceived and generated than ever before in this age of immediate communication. In order to enhance the world, new business owners are developing never-before-seen content and services as part of the current entrepreneurial wave. With so much going on, it's easy to develop something that's a little too similar to someone else. Fortunately, there are various options for dealing with copyright issues.

1. Ask the original owner for **permission**

When it comes to copyrighted content, the only legal method to utilize it is to contact the original owner and ask for their permission. If this isn't possible, there are websites such as Creative Commons that provide royalty-free image and audio materials that can be used commercially.

2. File a trademark and copyright application for your own work

It is critical to get legal rights to whatever you produce that you plan to turn into a business or cash stream. You cannot prohibit someone from coming up with a comparable idea and founding a business based on it, even if it is your intellectual property. It's critical to safeguard your ideas by trademarking and copyrighting them.

3. Obtain a copyright license.

Copyrighting intellectual property is as simple as putting the copyright symbol in front of it and signing your name. The

Copyright Act, on the other hand, includes those themes that are more difficult to establish ownership of, such as architectural and choreographic works. To legally claim ownership of your own work and prevent illicit copying, you should speak with a copyright lawyer.

4. Register your property as a trademark.

The primary difference between a trademark and a copyright is what it protects. While a copyright normally protects a creative work, trademarks protect names, logos, emblems, and other business intellectual property. Because trademarking a property is a lengthy and complicated procedure, it's essential to seek professional assistance. You must first search for trademarks that are similar to the one you intend to apply; even though an existing trademark isn't identical, a trademark that is too similar can prevent you from filing.

5. Keep in mind that registration isn't required.

In the United States, there has been no official necessity for copyrighted work to contain the copyright symbol since 1978. When a novel is 'saved' as a word document, for example, it is protected. However, while proprietary copyrighting provides some protections, registering the work does not. Only if a person's copyright is registered can they sue over a copyright issue. Damage restitution will only be calculated after the content has been registered, not before.

While it may seem like an extra step, copyrighting and trademarking your intellectual or physical property can protect it in ways that claiming ownership cannot. Copyright issues may cause a lot of headaches for content creators and those who want to use their work, but knowing how to deal with them before they happen can save a lot of time and money.

What Are the Most Common Forms of Intellectual Property?

Inventions, academic and creative works, patterns and markings, names and likenesses used in trade and business are all examples of intellectual property (IP). All intellectual property is protected by numerous laws in place on a local, regional, national, and international level. Patents, trademarks, copyright, service marks, trade secrets, and other intellectual property rights are all protected by law.

What is a patent?

A patent is an absolute right awarded for an invention, which is a product or a process that, in general, suggests a new specialized solution to a problem or gives a new way of doing something. In order to get a patent, a patent application must disclose methodological information about the invention to the public. Obtaining a patent is a difficult process. If you want to get a patent, you need to start by going to this website: The Patent and Trademark Office of the United States of America. You can file for a patent once you've gained a basic understanding of the process and the regulations that govern it. However, keep in mind that this is a complicated process, and hiring a patent attorney is the best way to go.

What exactly is copyright?

Copyright is a legal word that refers to the rights that authors and artists have over their works of literature and art. Books, music, paintings, sculpture, films, computer programs, databases, commercials, maps, technical drawings, and other works are all covered by copyright. Copyright is a simple IP to apply for, and most people can fill out a form and submit their work in a few minutes. To learn everything you need to know about applying for a copyright, including fees and what to submit, go to the Copyright Office's website: The Copyright Office of the United States of America

What is a trademark?

A trademark is a symbol that differentiates one company's goods or services from those of other companies. Patents and trademarks are protected by intellectual property laws. Trademark protection can be obtained by filing a trademark registration application with the trademark office and paying the applicable fees. The website for patents is the same.

What is the difference between a service mark and a trademark?

A service mark is a logo that differentiates one service from another. Businesses use service marks to link their services together and distinguish them from those offered by others in the same sector. Letters, words, symbols, and other devices are used as service marks to inform consumers about the origin or source of a certain service. The US Patent and Trademark Office (the "USPTO") is where you may register your trademark.

What is a Trade Secret?

A trade secret is defined as "knowledge, including a formula, pattern, compilation, program, gadget, method, technique, or process that provides independent economic value," according to the Uniform Trade Secrets Act ("UTSA"). These secrets are either palpable or imminent, and are largely unknown or difficult to find by those who would profit financially from their disclosure or use; they are the focus of efforts that are logical under the circumstances to maintain their concealment. The acquisition of the use of a trade secret is prohibited in two scenarios. There is legal standing for a lawsuit if a trade secret is obtained illegally or through a breach of confidence. Lawful methods of obtaining trade secrets include private discovery, reverse engineering, and unintended disclosure. Failure to take adequate protective steps by the trade secret owners may allow this to happen. Unfair competition is defined as the theft of trade secrets. As with computer programs, reverse engineering is frequently prohibited.

What is Industrial Design?

An industrial design right is a type of intellectual property that protects the visual design of non-functional goods. An industrial design is the construction of a three-dimensional model, pattern, or composition of a pattern or color, or permutation of a pattern and color that has aesthetic value. An industrial design is a two- or three-dimensional prototype used to manufacture a product, an industrial commodity, or a handcraft.

What is Trade Dress?

Trade dress is a legal term of art that refers to the elements of a product's image, packaging, or architectural design that indicate the product's source to consumers.

What is the definition of fair use?

Any partial reproduction of copyrighted material that changes the objective, such as to remark on, ridicule, or satirize a copyrighted work, is considered fair use. Without the authorization of the copyright owner, such uses are permissible. Fair use is a defense to a copyright infringement accusation.

Criticism and Commentary

Fair use principles allow you to recreate some of the work to accomplish your goals while commenting on or critiquing a copyrighted work, such as a book review or any other valid review.

The most frequent types of intellectual property are listed below. If you believe something you've made falls into one of the categories listed in this article, you should consider registering your work or product. Make sure what you're registering isn't the same as what someone else has previously done.

Resources

Copyright Agency Limited (CA) - pay for a licence to copy books, articles, essays and artwork.

Screenrights - educational institutions and government agencies can pay for a licence to copy or broadcast certain film, television and radio productions.

Publishers Global - find publishers listed by country. It has links to publishers in around 55 countries, including links to around 420 Australian publishers.

Firms Out of Business (FOB) - lists some of the international publishing firms, magazines, literary agencies and similar organisations that are no longer in existence.

Writers Artists and Their Copyright Holders (WATCH) - a useful source for contact details of international writers.

Chapter Five: In Copyright Infringement Cases, How Do You Respond To Settlement Letters?

Settlement letters are addressed to specific internet users who have been found to have infringed on a copyrighted piece of content. The letter, also known as a letter of demand (LOD), normally contains the infringer's name, IP address, and any relevant information concerning the copyright infringement. To begin with, receiving a demand letter such as a TCYK letter indicates that you have likely broken the law and that the copyright enforcers have evidence that you have infringed on protected information. Second, it is not wise to simply disregard the letter because this could result in serious legal ramifications. So, if you receive a demand letter, answer. In every case of unauthorized downloading, inquire about the situation or the letter's meaning. If you ever find yourself in a lawsuit as a "John Doe" defendant, here are some practical recommendations to assist you defending yourself:

- The amount of the settlement is frequently negotiable. If you receive a TCYK letter or any other type of settlement letter, you will almost certainly be offered a settlement amount. Depending on how you approach the situation or how you try to negotiate, the figure may fluctuate. So it wouldn't harm to give it a shot, especially if you were serious about it.
- Pornography is the most embarrassing and dangerous of the copyrighted products that you may possibly pirate. Therefore, find a means to settle promptly. Don't squander time putting off the case. It's

advisable to get rid of it as soon as it's presented to you.
- Never resist a subpoena. Doing so may result in your identity being revealed. Copyright violations are not something to be taken lightly. You must safeguard your personal identification in order to avoid a potential scandal that will not benefit you in any manner.
- In comparison to every negotiated settlement, fighting a case could result in higher costs. Aside from the inconvenience that a lawsuit might bring, there are legal expenditures to consider if you decide to pursue a case. If you merely settle, you can end up with a total that could have been avoided.

A copyright gives a creator exclusive rights to distribute or reproduce his original work, according to copyright law. There may be exceptions, but generally, the creator first owns the copyright to their work. It would be beneficial if people had a greater grasp of how artists create works of art, such as those in the entertainment business. In the meanwhile, they should concentrate on how to reply to a demand letter.

Copyright Registration's Benefits

When running a business, you must exercise caution and ensure that all of your company's interests are protected. When you create a product, launch a design, or even come up with a recommendation to improve what you're selling, it's critical that you copyright it. Without the proper copyright in place, anyone can utilize your recommendations or duplicate your designs. It will drain the profits from your company while also removing its exclusivity. Make sure you have a copyright registration completed to avoid this type of situation. There are numerous advantages to copyright registration; continue reading to learn more.

What is copyright?

Copyright is a legal term that refers to a certain type of intellectual property protection. It guards against plagiarism once your work has been rendered tangible, that is, given a physical form. A tale printed on paper, for example, will be copyrighted, but not a narrative concept.

What role does copyright play in your business?

In layman's terms, a copyright assures that no one else uses your work without your permission. And if someone uses it without your consent, you have the right to sue them.

Here's what you can do as a copyright owner:

- Reproduce the work
- Create other materials (spinoff work) based on the common
- Distribute your work via sale, rent, and even transfer of ownership
- Display the work (for example, if it's an art piece) You can also transfer these above-mentioned rights to anyone else via a contract.

The Benefits of Copyright Registration

Let's have a look at some of the most significant advantages of copyright registration:

- **Legal evidence:** Obtaining a copyright registration provides the most crucial and significant benefit. Your work is legally declared to be yours if you have a copyright in place. This keeps it non-toxic. And if someone copies or infringes on your design, plan, or product, you can use the registered copyright as evidence in court. This will almost certainly shift the scales in your favor automatically and quickly. You may find it difficult to challenge such a problem if you do not use copyright. However, if a copyright has been registered previously, such issues will be easily resolved.

- **Public notice:** We also have a lot of experience with copyright registration. While your work is copyrighted, it is documented in your title. Not only does this preserve your work, but it also gives you ownership and allows you to disseminate your name more widely in public. This gives your design or concept a face and believability. It also stops others from claiming ownership and falsely claiming to have invented or manufactured that particular body of work. Nobody can claim that they were unaware of your ownership and mistakenly claimed the work as their own. This can help you maintain your reputation as an expert in your field, which can lead to financial and honorable benefits.

- **Seeking damages:** Plagiarism is not only a threat to your small business's financial well-being, but it's also a threat to your reputation and status. So, if you find yourself in a copyright infringement tangle for any reason, you can seek damages against the culprits. However, if the copyright is safely registered in your name, this is more likely to happen. You won't be able to build your case unless you have that.

So, make a list of any potential future mishaps and register your copyright as soon as possible.

• **Early registration:** You'll have a few years to register the copyright, but it's still a good idea to take advantage of the early registration opportunity. This is necessary because if you procrastinate, someone else may swoop in and register anything as their identity. After then, despite being the lawful owner of your long-established design, proposal, or product, you will have no rights to it. It is quite simple to register your copyright in your own name. The procedure will also be done in a short amount of time online. So, don't wait for a disaster to come, because it'll usually be too late to return and mend your service provider's potentialities by then.

• **Assists you in standing out from the crowd:** At every turn in life, there is a fierce competitor. When you own a business, you may also find yourself lost in a multitude of competitors. Nonetheless, a copyright registration could come in handy in this situation. Even if it's a small object, copyrighting it makes it inaccessible to your competitors. This will make you stand out from the crowd and boost your revenue immediately. Don't overlook the importance of copyright registration while starting your own firm.

Getting your copyright registered is, without a doubt, the most important thing to accomplish. This modest endeavor of copyright registration provides you with a slew of advantages. You might get a lot out of it, from keeping your ideas reliable to bringing in more financial rewards. If you haven't yet registered your copyrights, you should do so right now!

Resources

©Guide | Know Your Copy Rights

This guide provides information about users' rights under copyright law. It is a printable PDF version of the Rights of Users page of our Copyright Basics guide.

©Guide | Copyright and Course Websites

This guide provides answers to common questions about copyright and course websites. It is a printable PDF version of our Copyright and Course Websites guide.

©Guide | Copyright and Using Video

This guide provides information about copyright and using video. It is a printable PDF version of our Copyright and Using Video guide.

©Guide | Copyright for Dissertations

This guide provides answers to common copyright questions for authors of dissertations at the University of Michigan. It is a printable version of our Copyright for Dissertations guide. It is a PDF.

Copyright Basics in Brief (Electronic Version)

This one-page PDF is a brief summary of the material covered by the Copyright Basics guide. This is the electronic version, with URLs labeled.

Chapter Six: Top 10 Reasons to Register Your Copyright

The act of creating a unique work of art automatically makes it yours and yours alone. It's your intellectual property, whether it's a distinctive beat, lyrics to a song, dance steps, or a TV pilot outline. This asset, like real estate or a bank account, is valuable and should be safeguarded. Certainly, you should be the one to become renowned as a result of your musical ideas or profit handsomely from their sale, not the guy who plagiarized them.

No one would steal intellectual property and claim it as their own in a perfect society. Even in a perfect environment, humans can inadvertently and independently create functionally similar works of art. At the very least, proving that you created the work of art first would be challenging. Nonetheless, just as there are vaults for storing money and documents for proving ownership of land, the law provides a simple means to safeguard your intellectual property: copyright registration. Here are the 10 reasons to register a copyright, with apologies to David Letterman and in no particular order:

1. A copyright registration notifies the rest of the world. It's your legal declaration to the world that you own particular intellectual property and that making unauthorized copies is against the law. Would-be thieves are warned that stealing your ideas is at their own peril if they register.

2. A copyright registration safeguards your intellectual property from accidental but unauthorized copying. The famous case of David Bowie suing Vanilla Ice for copyright infringement over the hook to "Ice, Ice Bay" is a good

example of this. Even though Vanilla Ice claimed he copied the rhythm accidentally (a claim he later denied), he still owed David Bowie money for using it without authorization.

3. Credit is given where it is due when a copyright is registered. This is proof that you, and not someone else, are the creator of a work of art. Registration upholds a fundamental ideal that has nothing to do with money.

4. A copyright registration allows you to claim statutory damages and attorney's expenses. To put it another way, suing for statutory damages eliminates the need to establish that you were harmed by a copyright violation. A typical lawsuit necessitates the demonstration of injury. For an intentional violation, you can sue for up to $150,000, and for an unintentional violation, you can sue for up to $30,000. If you want to claim statutory damages, you must register your copyright within three months of making it public.

5. In copyright infringement litigation, a registered copyright gives strong evidence that you own specific intellectual property. This means that the plaintiff must prove that no violation happened; otherwise the case will be dismissed.

6. If you have a registered copyright, you can register it with US Customs. In turn, US Customs will safeguard you from illicit copies imported from other nations.

7. A copyright registration allows you to prevent unauthorized copies from being made. You can get a court order requiring an infringing party to stop infringing on your property. When record labels sued Napster, this is exactly what happened.

8. To litigate for copyright infringement, you must have a copyright that has been registered. You must be a player in order to benefit from the system. By registering your copyright under copyright laws, you obtain important legal protection.

9. A copyright that has been registered offers legal protection even after the owner has died. Copyright laws in the United States frequently result in your copyright being enforced even after you've passed away. Although you can't take your wealth to heaven, it's crucial for someone who wishes to leave a legacy for their loved ones.

10. Copyright registration saves time and money. Even if you don't have a registered copyright, you can sue someone for stealing your intellectual property; it's simply not a smart idea. Waving a copyright certificate rather than scrawled lyrics on a napkin tends to go over better in court for some reason. When an attorney is required, registering a copyright makes the legal process considerably easier and less expensive.

The following is a list of my top ten reasons for registering a copyright. But that doesn't mean there are only ten reasons or that we can all agree on which ones are the most significant. What are some other reasons to register a copyright, and why do you believe one is more significant than the other?

How to Avoid Copyright Violations

People can protect their intellectual property in a variety of ways, including copyright, patents, trademarks, and trade secrets. However, there are significant distinctions between each of the protective instruments in terms of what they protect.

Copyright is one of the most common instruments utilized in intellectual property issues. "Original works of authorship, including literary, dramatic, musical, and creative works, such as poetry, novels, movies, songs, computer software, and architecture," according to the government's Copyright office. It does not, however, safeguard "... facts, ideas, systems, or operational procedures." In layman's words, a "C" inside of a circle (indicating Copyright) can be found in books, CDs, video games, and even theater scripts.

The purpose of this type of intellectual property legislation is to protect the creator. You could be a victim of copyright infringement without even realizing it. As a result, it's a good idea to brush up on how to follow the guidelines when working with the stamp. It's worth noting that even if a work doesn't display the copyright sign, it may still be protected by the law. "The author or creator retains the rights to the work and can decide if and how others use his or her production," writes Legalzoom, describing the concept of copyright. It's particularly illegal if you use someone else's copyrighted work for profit or commercial gain. Legalzoom also provides a few examples of copyright infringement that may appear to consumers to be harmless but are actually prohibited.

Obtaining movies and music without paying for their use:

- Movies are being recorded in the theater.
- Using other people's photos on a blog without their permission
- Copying software without giving credit where credit is due is unethical.
- Using unlicensed music clips in videos
- Unauthorized copies of books, blogs, or podcasts

Anything in which you are plagiarizing someone else's original work without their permission.

If you've ever browsed YouTube, you've most likely came across an amateur singer doing a version of a popular song. It's technically copyright infringement if the amateur artist did not obtain authorization from the original songwriter. Will a famous person pursue a lawsuit over a singer's video with ten views? He or she is unlikely to do so, although it is possible. Taking the risk isn't a good idea because big firms sometimes use software that can troll the Internet for the sole goal of looking for copyright infringement cases.

You should be cautious about how you use an artistic expression that you did not create in order to prevent copyright infringement. Whether or not the copyright symbol appears, you should always assume that if you use someone else's work without permission or credit, the owner will take legal action against you.

Some artists or writers are more than ready to share their work with the rest of the world, but first do your research. These agreements are typically in the form of licenses, which allow consumers to use the work subject to certain rules and restrictions.

There's no need to worry about the picture you used in your slide show last week if you're using the piece of art for instructional purposes. There is an exception known as "fair use," which permits what would otherwise be considered infringement if the usage was for a non-commercial reason.

Resources

Copyright Basics in Brief (Printable Version)

This one-page PDF is a brief summary of the material covered by the Copyright Basics guide. This is the printable version, with URLs visible.

Finding the Public Domain: Copyright Review Management System Toolkit

This toolkit describes our effort to conduct copyright review of books at a large scale.

Notice for Unsupervised Copying Equipment

US copyright law does not impose liability for copyright infringement upon a library or archives or its employees for the unsupervised use of reproducing equipment located on its premises, so long as the equipment displays a notice that the making of a copy may be subject to copyright law. Our notice reminds our patrons of their responsibilities and rights. It is a PDF.

Codes of Best Practices in Fair Use

These codes document the shared best practices of communities that rely on fair use, including fair use for online video, fair use of images for teaching, research, and study, fair use for OpenCourseWare, fair use for documentary filmmakers, fair use for the visual arts, and fair use for academic and research libraries.

Copyright Crash Course

The University of Texas Libraries maintain this resource on the basics of copyright.

Chapter Seven: Protect Your Work With Copyrights

Original works of authorship that remain constant in a tangible shape, whether published or unpublished, are protected by copyright. Artwork, literary works, live performances, photographs, movies, and software programs are all examples of works that may be protected by copyright laws.

It's important to remember that copyright law only protects the "form of the expression" of a work, not the actual principles, thoughts, methods, or data included within it. This is the reason why a work must remain consistent in a tangible form in order to obtain copyright protection. Testimonies written on paper and original artwork on canvas are two examples of works that are stable in a tangible form.

What is a copyright, exactly? Copyright protection is often applied to literary works, musicals, artwork, sculptures, and other creative works. A copyright protects the shape of an expression rather than the subject that the expression depends on. The artworks must contain some aspect of originality and ingenuity.

What am I allowed to do with my copyright? The owner of a copyright has exclusive rights to reproduce, assemble derivative works, distribute copies, perform publicly, and/or exhibit copyrighted works.

What can I do to defend myself? "Authentic works of authorship fixed in any tangible medium of expression...," according to the judicial code. You could wonder what distinguishes anything as a "original design." "Original" means that the creator did not copy someone else's work exactly and that there are at least a few modest degrees of innovation involved.

There is no longer any need for official registration to "protect" your work. So, why do people register for copyrights in the first place? To protect your copyright, you must register formally. This is how you'll be able to register with the copyright office, which will then go to court to enforce your copyrights. It's required to prevent someone from plagiarizing your work.

Furthermore, correct copyright registration enables you to sign in the copyrighted work, allowing you to prevent infringing works from being created.

I'd want to plagiarize someone else's work. Is that possible? It's fantastic to be genuine. However, there are specific circumstances in which you may utilize another person's artwork, and this is where the Fair Use Doctrine comes into play. This is a complicated and fact-based assessment. In general, you'll be able to use the elements of a copyrighted work if you're criticizing a piece of work, commenting, news reporting, teaching, or creating a parody. The safest bet is to ask the copyright owner for permission to use a piece of their work. Remember that simply providing credit to the original author isn't enough to avoid copyright infringement accusations.

Ensuring That You Own Your Content's Copyright

You've been a productive writer for your company for a long time, and you use sources to back up the facts you publish in your material, just like any other writer. Of course, you have no reason to believe anything other than the fact that you own the copyright to everything you're writing.

The line can be blurred at times.

You can do whatever you want with a piece of work if you own the copyright to it (including graphics, videos, and other media). It is, after all, your property. If someone else owns the copyright to the content, you are severely limited in what you can do with it. That means you can't reuse the material, but you can allow others to post it on their websites (for better exposure and reach), and you can't change the images (making them smaller, larger, wider, narrower). In that situation, your options are limited. However, you may not always recognize when it is appropriate (legally and ethically) to make any changes to the text and when you should stay away.

You probably have a good idea that you can't just go online and locate a graphic image to copy and paste into your material. It's only common sense. If you use any part of someone else's material (words), you're probably aware that you must credit the author for his or her work. The copyright, on the other hand, extends well beyond that. It's critical that you grasp the fundamentals of copyright and how they apply to you and your company. You can get into problems if you don't pay attention to what you're allowed and what you're not allowed to do (legally and financially speaking). There are some principles that will help you if you have a basic understanding of them. Hopefully, they will not apply to you at any point in the future, but being aware is critical.

Have a licensing agreement in place, along with an invoice: That is a copyright invoice from the owner of the copyright. If you intend to use material for which another person (or entity) holds the copyright, you will almost certainly have to pay that person (or entity) money. It is possible that the person or entity will not charge you money in rare situations, but you must have a documented agreement in order to avoid getting into difficulty.

Copyright infringement lawsuit: This is a case that takes place in federal court. The owner of the copyright is the person or entity who is suing. The complaint will make demands, such as removing all copyrighted information from all online locations where it has been uploaded. You will also (most certainly) be required to pay a sum of money (damages), and you may be compelled to pay the lawyers' expenses.

Cease-and-desist communication: This is a communication from the copyright owner (typically in the form of a letter) instructing you that you must remove their content from wherever you have placed it.

Takedown notice for the Digital Millennium Copyright Act: This is a notice that refers to the act on behalf of the copyright owner. It's delivered to your web hosting provider. It will demand that your web hosting service block all access to the copyrighted information wherever it exists.

The worrying aspect of this predicament is that, depending on the copyright owner's whims, you could find yourself paying in a variety of ways. It could be trivial, but it could also be serious. The copyright violation may be notified to you in phases. If you answer as soon as possible after receiving the first notice, you might get lucky and, after doing whatever is required of you, that will be the end of it, as long as you never do it again. If you persist, though, the effects will almost certainly get more severe. If you want to get out of this position reasonably undamaged, you'll need to step carefully and accomplish whatever you need to do swiftly.

Learn about your legal rights.

When you're first writing a piece of content, you should take precautions to ensure that you don't run into any of the issues listed above. If you aren't the one who created the content, you must obtain copyright ownership from the other party. It's vital that you get it down on paper. The best thing you can do is have a formal contract with the other party. Hopefully, there will be no doubt about anything in such a scenario. It's best to include this in the contract as well if you want the creator to profit from the work. You'll want to include topics like what's being made, how modifications are handled, deadlines and the repercussions if those deadlines are missed, the payment plan, who owns the copyright, and who is accountable for the consequences if the copyright is violated in the contract. If you've had a long-term connection with that person, you'll almost certainly need to modify your contract at some point.

You may not have thought about copyright ownership very frequently (or at all); yet, you must keep it in mind at all times and be conscious of doing the right thing. If you don't, the results will almost certainly be unpleasant. At all times, you must safeguard your reputation as well as your bank account. Copyright rules are extremely complex, and you may not even be aware that you are breaking them. However, you must be careful of your actions and ensure that you are not infringing on any copyright laws. Surprisingly, there are a few instances where you don't require permission from the content's copyright owner. You should conduct research to discover when those restrictions apply, which will alleviate some of the load. Obviously, you had no idea you were doing anything illegal. However, if you are aware, you must ensure that you follow all of the rules.

Resources

Cornell University Copyright Information Center

Cornell's copyright website includes a handy chart for determining whether a work is in the public domain in the United States.

Create Change

The Association of Research Libraries and the Scholarly Publishing and Academic Resources Coalition developed this site to explain scholarly communication issues in the digital realm.

Cross-Border Copyright Guide 2017

This free guide from TerraLex provides overviews of copyright law in 18 countries, written by local experts.

Fair Use for Nonfiction Authors

This guide, published by the Authors Alliance, explains when fair use applies to the use of sources in nonfiction works such as scholarly articles. It has been endorsed by the American Council of Learned Societies and the Association for Information Science and Technology.

Model Publishing Contract for Digital Scholarship

The Model Publishing Contract was developed "to facilitate the publication of open access books, including accommodating new types of long-form, multimodal digital scholarship."

Chapter Eight: How to Acquire Copyright for a Book

One of the most common inquiries young writers have is how to get their book copyrighted. It's a crucial question as well. While the majority of writers do not have their work stolen or copied, it does happen, and the greatest defense is preparation.

Many people are unaware that your work is "copyrighted" the moment you create it; it is only yours. It is yours and you have legal ownership once your work is in a concrete form (written down in the case of literary work).

Regrettably, this is a legally ambiguous safeguard. Although you are aware that you own it, a court may require proof that you have registered the copyright.

Copyright registration establishes your legal ownership of the work. While you immediately own the work, copyrighting (or, more precisely, registering the copyright) provides the legal proof you'll need in the event of a dispute.

If you are a victim of plagiarism, you must first have the copyright registered before you can file a lawsuit. Your claim is strengthened by the fact that you registered the copyright as soon as the work was finished or released.

How to Register

Copyright registration is straightforward and inexpensive.

When you've finished your book, go to the US Copyright Office and get a copyright form (www.copyright.gov). The

Copyright Office's website can assist you in determining which of the three forms you require for copyrighting literary works.

The form, a $50 copyright registration fee, and one copy of your work in its "best edition" must all be submitted. If you're copyrighting an unpublished work, send a copy of the manuscript; if the work is already published, send the hardcover edition if one exists.

You may also register for $35 by going to their website. Go to copyright.gov and select electronic.

Your certificate could take anywhere from nine to 22 months to arrive.

Scams to Avoid

Because copyright is much easier than many people understand, there are many unscrupulous people waiting to take advantage of those who don't know how to copyright their work. For a price, these con artists will offer to "copyright" your work for you.

You don't need to engage a copyright agent, and you don't need to pay someone to handle your copyright registration. Some of the agents that offer this service are trustworthy; others are not, and some have been accused of registering copyrights in their own names. All of them, on the other hand, offer to do anything for a fee. This is something you can do on your own.

Copyright registration should be a component of your publication procedure. If you work with a publisher, be sure the copyright is registered in your name rather than theirs.

Copyright registration should be nearly automatic for all writers now that copyright registration is so easy.

How to Copyright a Book - 4 Tips to Protect Your Novel

Copyright protection for your book can be very simple and quick. It's also become much more economical than in the past, thanks to the proliferation of internet copyright registries.

Tip 1: Determine whether your book is copyrighted.

Before you can use copyright to protect your book, you must first decide whether it comes into one of the categories that copyright covers. Because it is a nondramatic textual work expressed using words, numbers, or symbols and may or may not have images, a book would fit under "Literary Works."

Tip 2: Originality is required for copyrighted books

Your book must not be a straight copy of someone else's work in order to be labeled 'original.' This does not, however, exclude your book from being based on someone else's work or from being a derivative work, as both are permitted under copyright law.

To be unique, the work must incorporate some element of inventiveness. In other words, if you were to put up a recipe collection, the sequence and types of recipes you chose would have to be unique, and thus would be protected under copyright law. Copyright law does not protect the literal listing of ingredients, but it does protect the precise representation of the procedures, directions, hints, and ideas for serving.

In other types of books, the story thread does not have to be original. However, the actual expression (words and sentences) of the story must be yours and not copied. To put it another way, there may be a thousand books written about online copyright procedures (a broad topic); but, each author can claim the copyright to their book's precise expression.

Tip 3: Make your book tangible to protect it.

Now that you've determined that your book qualifies for copyright protection, you'll need to put it in a format that allows for copyright protection. The book must be put in a fixed form in order to qualify as a literary work under copyright law. To establish a 'fixed form' of your book, simply write it down on paper or save it to your computer. To put it another way, once you've generated a concrete version of your work, it's considered 'fixed' and hence protected under copyright law.

Tip 4: Choose a copyright registry for your book

Your work will be immediately protected under copyright law if you complete the steps mentioned above. If infringement occurs, however, proving you are the book's original creator may be challenging. As a result, many authors opt to have their books registered with a copyright registry.

Note that US people can register their book with any copyright registry, but they must register with the US Copyright Office if they intend to pursue their claim to court. Non-US citizens are exempt from this rule. Having said that, most copyright infringement cases are settled out of court once the infringing party sees the proof provided by the registration.

To find a copyright register, simply search for "protect copyright" on a search engine and pick one from the results. Ensure that the registry you choose has no hidden fees and that it will safeguard your book for the duration of its copyright (50-70 years). If infringement occurs, you can be assured that you have the proof required by the courts to show your ownership of the book.

Disclaimer: The preceding information is provided as a general reference to help you learn more about copyright. It is not intended to be legal advice. You should consult a copyright lawyer in your country if you have any questions regarding your unique work.

Resources

Stanford Copyright and Fair Use Website

The Stanford University Libraries offer a comprehensive site that includes "primary case law, statutes, regulations, as well as current feeds of newly filed copyright lawsuits, pending legislation, regulations, copyright office news, scholarly articles, blog and twitter feeds from practicing attorneys and law professors."

Stanford Copyright Renewal Database

This database searches Library of Congress copyright renewal records for books published from 1923 to 1963.

Tales from the Public Domain: BOUND BY LAW?

This comic from the Center for the Study of the Public Domain at Duke Law School tells the story of a documentary filmmaker facing copyright-related obstacles.

Teaching Copyright

The Electronic Frontier Foundation created this curriculum to help teachers educate students about copyright.

United States Copyright Office

On the US Copyright Office's site, you can register your copyrights, search copyright records, and learn more about copyright law.

Chapter Nine: Tips to Choose The Best Copyright Lawyer

Copyrights are an essential component of any business. Any country's copyright laws are dedicated to protecting artists' various creations, ranging from art, music, and any other constructive idea, and allowing them to reap various rewards from their work. In this era of technological transformation, many copyright laws are being updated to protect the rights of creators. In this context, we may state that copyright cases are intricate and necessitate the use of appropriate resources in order to reach a fair conclusion.

If you've filed a copyright case as a first step, you'll need a qualified copyright lawyer to help you with the rest of the process. Here are some suggestions for selecting the finest copyright attorney for your case.

Know your requirements: The best method to hire a copyright lawyer is to first understand your requirements. Copyright is a wide topic that covers a lot of ground. So, if you're an author who wants to protect both your publishing and financial rights, you'll need a copyright lawyer. Similarly, if you believe your copyright has been infringed upon, you can seek legal advice from a copyright lawyer.

Select a copyright lawyer based on your needs: Once you've determined your needs, find a copyright lawyer with experience in the field. A few examples will help you grasp this concept more clearly. If you're being sued under copyright law, you'll want to hire a lawyer who has experience defending clients. Similarly, if an infringement is necessary, hire the top lawyer in the industry to assist you in obtaining damages. If you only wish to register your recent creative work under copyright law, however, seek out a copyright attorney who specializes in this area.

Determine the ability: Copyright works include literary works, dramatic works such as mime or dance, musical works, creative works, film, and so on. As a result, each attorney or lawyer specializes in a specific form of invention. Some lawyers specialize in dealing with written creative works, while others specialize in the Internet. It is usually a good idea to seek the advice of a law company that specializes in various disciplines. This will make it easier for you to cope with copyright issues.

Use the internet for assistance: Look through several websites to learn more about lawyers who specialize in a particular subject. There are various websites that provide past experience and comprehensive reviews of their work depending on their distinct fields of competence. You can obtain all of their contact information in order to contact them directly or at their offices. You can acquire a professional copyright lawyer in this manner without spending your valuable time or money. Aside from the Internet, you can get referrals from friends and coworkers before obtaining expert assistance.

Thus, the ideal strategy to hire copyright lawyers is to conduct extensive study into the relevant sector and select the best. Without a doubt, the process is time-consuming, but it will undoubtedly assist you in obtaining the finest available offer. Because copyright concerns are sensitive, and often a person's entire career and financial rewards are at stake, the selection procedure must be rigorous and specific.

5 Ways To Stay Away From Copyright Infringement On Social Media

The use of websites and programs to stay socially connected and share user-generated content on the internet is known as social media. This content may include images, written work, and reports, among other things. Online sharing of various forms of media is possible with social networking sites. As a result, social media becomes a battleground for copyright infringement. The content that is shared on business accounts is usually for marketing objectives. Businesses often overlook the danger of being sued for exploiting copyrighted information online while developing relevant content. Suits for copyright infringement can typically be avoided by a conscientious business owner. Here are a few pointers to keep in mind if you want to prevent having to deal with content ownership issues.

1) Obtain permission.

Obtaining the author's permission is the best way to use copyrighted content. If you're using an image, you may find out who created it by looking at the watermark or following any links supplied. If you get permission, you can use the content, give the original author credit, and link it to your post. To stay out of trouble, keep track of the permissions you acquire.

2) Make use of images that are in the public domain.

Use photos from sites with no copyright limitations whenever possible. Pixabay, Wikimedia Commons, Creative Commons, Pexels, and Feerange, to mention a few, provide photos with no copyright limitations for use. These websites have photographs on a wide range of themes that you may use to create content. This is a relatively simple technique to avoid copyright difficulties.

3) Acknowledge others.

Many people believe that using copyrighted content as long as they provide acknowledgment in their post is OK. Even if you have given credit to the concerned individual in your social media post, you might still be sued by the author without prior approval.

4) Investigate Who Owns What on Social Media Pages.

Copyrighted content is strictly prohibited on any social media account. It's a good idea to go over all of your social media profiles' ownership rights policies. Each social networking platform follows its own set of guidelines.

5) Consider purchasing content.

Buying copyrighted content is a surefire strategy to keep your firm out of legal trouble. It is always preferable to invest in resources rather than pay a fortune to avoid lawsuits and penalties. There are numerous websites where you can buy materials for a small fee. Some websites that allow you to purchase photographs for use include Shutterstock, Bigstock, and iStock.

Resources

Fair Use Evaluator
Tool: http://librarycopyright.net/resources/fairuse/index.php

Copyright Clearance Center
http://www.copyright.com

U.S. Copyright Office
http://www.copyright.gov/

Know Your Copyrights (Association of Research Libraries)
Know Your Copyrights website

Cornell University Law School: Copyright Overview
http://www.law.cornell.edu/topics/copyright.html

Chapter Ten: How To Obtain Copyright Permission?

Permission is typically required before using someone else's copyrighted work. There are several exceptions, such as where the usage is covered by a statutory license or is in the public domain and hence regarded as a fair use. However, because the question is about how to obtain permission (with the exception of works that have entered the public domain as a result of the expiration of the copyright term, which is briefly discussed below), we'll assume that the user has already performed this analysis and determined that permission to use the work is required.

Step One: Figure out what kind of permission you'll require

Copyright laws grant exclusive rights to each inventor. Reproduction, distribution, modification, and public performance and display are all included under these rights. The creator has complete control over who receives these rights and how they are distributed. If the author wants his book published in the United States, he could give the rights to a US publisher; a Mexican publisher would get the rights to translate and distribute the book in Mexico; and a US movie studio would get the rights to make a film adaptation based on his book. You must know what kind of permission you need before asking for it, so you know what to say and who to approach.

I believe this is particularly relevant to music. There are two types of copyrighted works in music: musical compositions (which include lyrics and a musical score) and sound recordings (which include the sound itself) (what you actually hear on the radio). Your desired use may necessitate obtaining permission from several proprietors. You may also require multiple types of licenses, depending on the use. If you intend to record and distribute a cover version of a song, you'll need a mechanical license. The Harry Fox Agency is in charge of handling a large number of these permits. Performance rights organizations (PROs, such as ASCAP, BMI, SESAC, and GMR) give public performance licenses in exchange for money if you intend to perform the music (for example in live performance). When a musical work serves as the soundtrack to a video, film, or television show, synchronization (or "synch") permits are required.

Asking yourself the following questions can help you determine what kind of permission you require: Do you know what you're getting into? What permissions from the copyright owner do you require? Do you require those rights in any particular area? Is exclusivity important to you? When will you be able to use those privileges? Who do you want to reach with this message? What distribution plan do you have in place for your work? How much money do you have to spend?

Step Two: You need to find the copyright owners

Since permission to use a copyrighted work can only be granted by the copyright owner or the copyright owner's agent, finding the copyright owner is the first step (s). It's critical to realize that the copyright holder (s) and the creator (s) may or may not be the same person. Copyright ownership interests may have been transferred from the original inventor to a third party. When an author sells his copyright to a publisher, he may transfer ownership to the publisher, or a songwriter may have left her copyright ownership interests to a family member when she died. Copyright ownership can also be transferred or divided among multiple separate people. Since only the copyright owner (s) may grant you permission to use the work, you must begin your search for them rather than the person who created it.

A quick remark about discovering the rightful owner (s) of the work: When we talk about being able to "find" the copyright owner, what we truly mean is that we can connect with them. Copyright owners should be able to be contacted via phone or email if necessary. You don't have to know where they live to be able to help them.

As an aside, if you're not sure who developed an older work, you should find out because knowing the inventor will assist you in determining if the work's copyright protection term has expired. Due to the fact that the term for many copyrighted works is calculated by the creator's life plus an additional 70 years, knowing whether or not the creator died will help you determine when the work will expire into the public domain and thus if you need to seek permission at all fall. However, older works and corporate-sourced works (commonly referred to as "works done for hire") are referred to differently under copyright law.

It's important to realize that locating and identifying the copyright owner can be a very difficult task in many cases, so let's start with the basics. Many papers have been written on how to obtain authorization, and search firms are available to individuals who are interested in learning more. Meanwhile, the purpose of this discussion is to clarify the procedure for you and to provide you with assistance in starting. However, it's not meant to be a complete or indepth analysis of the subject.

Copyrighted works should always be checked first for three things: (1) a copyright notice; (2) any other evidence of copyright ownership; and (3) any information that could lead you to the copyright owner. Another option is to conduct a search in the United States Copyright Office's database. It's difficult to search the database, but the information on who owns the work should be there if it was registered with the Office. As long as owners haven't notified us of any changes, information in the database may be out-of-date.

Search engines on the internet are also beneficial. Utilize the searchable databases provided by different licensing agencies, trade and professional organizations, and relevant publishers and other organizations, such as the Copyright Clearance Center, based on the sort of work you intend to use. You can do so here. Guides on best practices in your business and at your local library may be of use. Visit the Copyright Alliance's "find a copyright owner" page for more information and access to useful resources.

Step Three: Negotiating Permission

Then you can get in touch with the copyright holder and start the process of getting permission and negotiating usage rights. This means that the copyright holder doesn't owe you an answer if you contact them. After finding the copyright owner and contacting them, but getting no answer, the work is not yours. Instead, you'll have to enlist the assistance of the property's proprietor. It's their prerogative to refuse your request if they so desire.

Exclusivity, territoriality, and duration of use are all important things to discuss, but you should also discuss payment conditions as well. Royalty payments are typically made as a one-time sum or as recurring payments. Numerous variables, such as the parties involved and the type of use, might influence payment amounts and timing. Copyright owners may not seek payment if the use is minimal enough. Alternatively, the use could give the copyright owner so much attention or expose them to a new audience that they opt to provide it free of charge.

Finally, make sure that whatever arrangement you have with the copyright owner is in writing. There will be no misunderstandings if everything is in paper now.

Resources

Special Issues

American Library Association – TEACH Act
http://www.ala.org/advocacy/copyright/teachact

BitLaw: A Resource for Technology Law
https://www.bitlaw.com

Music Publishers' Association Copyright Resource Center
http://www.mpa.org/copyright-resource-center/

NCSU TEACH Act Toolkit: Copyright & Distance Education
https://www.lib.ncsu.edu/cdsc/copyright/instruction/exceptions

WIPO (World Intellectual Property Organization)
http://www.wipo.int

Conclusion

Copyright can be found in a variety of works, including:

- "Literary work" refers to anything that is written, spoken, or sung, as well as a table or compilation, a computer program, or a database.
- "Dramatic work" refers to a piece of dance or mime.
- A "musical work" is a piece of music that is not accompanied by words or actions.
- "Artistic works" include any graphic work, such as a painting, drawing, diagram, map, chart, or plan, as well as any architectural work, such as a building or any work of artistic workmanship.
- 'Sound recording' refers to any sound recording that can be played back.
- The term "film" refers to any type of watchable moving image.
- A "broadcast" is any electronic transfer of visual images, sounds, or other data.
- 'Published editions' refers to the work's typographical arrangement and design, and often refers to the style, composition, layout, and overall appearance of a page in a published book.

"There is no provision in the copyright law regarding any such sort of protection," according to the US Copyright Office, "and it is not a replacement for registration." You won't have to register your work again once it's been published if you register it before it's published.

Even if you do not register your work, you may display the Copyright sign or symbol to demonstrate to the public that you are aware of your rights in it.

If your copyright is violated, you have the legal right to sue the person or company who is guilty. You must ensure that their usage constitutes an infringement, as the Copyright Act contains provisions that allow people to use copyrighted content without obtaining authorization.

www.ingramcontent.com/pod-product-compliance
Lightning Source LLC
Chambersburg PA
CBHW071316110426
42743CB00042B/2595